Mornings in The Word

Tammy L. Mashburn

Copyright © 2018 Tammy L. Mashburn

All rights reserved.

ISBN: 1984907891
ISBN-13: 978-1984907899

No part of this publication may be reproduced, stored in a retrieval system, or transmitted in any form, without prior written permission.

Cover Photo by: Debby Hudson

DEDICATION

Mornings in The Word was birthed out of my relationship with God. My years of a shallow relationship led to a longing for deeper relationship.

This book is for the women who have gone before me, who walk along beside me, and behind me. My longing is for you to find deep and abiding relationship in God.

CONTENTS

	Acknowledgments	i
1	Seek His Face	1
2	Lingering in the Secret and the Sacred	Pg 5
3	Real Life Highs and Lows	Pg 9
4	Stirrings	Pg 13
5	Tending My Garden	Pg 17
6	Know His Voice	Pg 21
7	Hearing or Telling	Pg 25
8	Do You Know Me	Pg 29
9	Sleeping on the Job	Pg 33
10	Heart Matters	Pg 37
11	Desperate for Jesus	Pg 41
12	Grace in Hollow Places	Pg 45
13	Broken Before the Cry	Pg 49
14	Seeking and Searching	Pg 52

15	Do Your Work and Stop Comparing	Pg 55
16	The Cost of Idolatry	Pg 59
17	Characteristics of Spiritual Growth	Pg 64
18	Fighting for Your Soul	Pg 69
19	Finding Life in the Valley of the Dry Bones	Pg 74
20	Clothed in Christ	Pg 78
21	Pride	Pg 82
22	Calm in the Storm	Pg 86
23	Sink or Swim: Jumping Overboard	Pg 90
24	Freedom: Caught in the Net	Pg 94
25	Hoarder or Giver	Pg 99
26	Looking Beyond the Closed Door	Pg 103
27	Run Your Race	Pg 107
28	Guide To Living In Your Abundance	Pg 111
29	Living Our Fullest Potential	Pg 115
30	Deep Roots	Pg 118
31	Feeding Your Soul	Pg 122
	About the Author	Pg 125

ACKNOWLEDGMENTS

First and foremost, I want to thank Susan Shipe. Without Susan, this little book would not be in your hands.

To my Women's Ministry Team and Prayer Warriors at View Church, you have prayed me through the pages. I love you to pieces.

To my Soul Sister who kept us in soup and brownies, and loves me in spite of my quirky ways.

And, lastly, My Sweet Man who has graciously survived many pajama days and no home-cooked meals. You love me well. I am blessed to do life with you.

1 SEEK HIS FACE

"My heart says this about you:
'Seek his face.'
Lord, I will seek your face."
Psalm 27:8

My Bible, journal, and pen wait for me as I move from bed to coffee pot and to my desk. This is what saves me from myself, my ambitions, and selfishness. It is the breath in my lungs and my survival in weary places. I come to life in the dark morning. Sitting in His presence, turning pages, seeking His face and calling out His name. The more I show up, the more I learn about God, His character, provision, and love for me.

There are glimpses of glory, glimpses of who He is shaping me to be.

We were created to be in relationship with our Father. We were created to be all that He means for us to be. If we do not show up, how do we know these things? If not the things of Jesus, what are we filling ourselves with?

The world beckons to us with relentless pursuit and glittery things, the need for more, and the need to be seen. Meanwhile our closets run over, our calendars over-fill, and our schedules squeeze the life out of us.

There is no space to live well or love well, much less pursue the God who created us to be in fellowship with Him. We close the gap between what we need and what we want with more. Our spinning lives and broken hearts are empty while appearing full. We paste a smile on our face and tell anyone who asks we are okay while inside we are shattering a million different ways.

What is the answer? How do we slow our spinning days?

Yet He often withdrew to deserted places and prayed. Luke 5:16

We follow Jesus into a deserted place and spend time with Him; we carve out space and a time to read and meditate on His Word. We set aside time to pray and commune with Him.

We live in a fast-food, expedited shipping world, where most of our needs are dropped at our door in forty-eight hours or less. Somewhere in the midst of it, we have lost the art of lingering. We have forgotten where and how to plant deep roots.

How we cultivate our relationship with Christ determines how, and what, we cultivate in every other part of our lives.

Journaling Prompt
What needs to change in my life in order to create space to cultivate time in the Word?

How can I spend time in the secret and sacred place with God?

2 LINGERING IN THE SECRET AND THE SACRED

Today, I am prone to linger. I can stretch my morning coffee for hours, take small bites of breakfast cookies while driving my Sweet Man's patience over the edge. If we need to leave early, I know to turn the alarm back, accommodating my slower ways.

Before P.O.T.S., not so much. I marched to the tune of the ticking clock with time clawing at my soul. Checking off the list, filling in space with more and more until I found myself depleted. Martha and I could have been best friends.

"Martha, Martha, you are worried and upset about many things." Luke 10:41 (CSB) The words singe me.

Sound familiar? Are you the same? Maybe you have experienced a major life change that brought with it the necessity to slow? Or, maybe, *unlike me,* you made the decision to slow before you crashed.

My life today looks different. I still fight my inner Martha. P.O.T.S. has given me no choice but to slow. I have become one who lingers. It's in this time of contemplation, this time of dark mornings spent bent over His Word, I come alive. I am transformed somehow.

Ecclesiastes 8:1 (CSB), says this, "A person's wisdom brightens his face." Where does wisdom come from? King Solomon tells us in Proverbs 2:6, wisdom comes from the Lord.

Lingering brings freedom and a lightness to my soul and changes my countenance.

The dirty truth I would rather sweep under the rug, unseen, is that I suffer from spiritual ADD. Easily distracted, eyes darting to the crumbs on the countertop, the laundry basket, and my phone; my heart stays one or two steps ahead of where I am. I fret the details of my day and I long to forget them and sit at the feet of my Beloved. I want to stop the noise, which circles around my mind.

"He made us, and we are his – his people, the sheep of his pasture." Psalm 100:3 (CSB)

He made me, He made you, one would think we could make time for sitting at His feet. Sitting in His presence, allowing the things of the world to fade away. For just a bit, letting go of the details, the pressing to-do list and linger. Linger in His presence.

When I look back to where I have been, and where He has brought me, I cannot help but linger in His presence. Feasting on the crumbs, seeking a banquet, and a heart opened to His faithfulness.

Transformation takes place when we invest time with God.

Journaling Prompt
How does spending time alone with God change you?

Does your day look different when you invest in this time?

3 REAL LIFE HIGH'S AND LOW'S

Have you ever experienced a moment where life's alignments are *near* perfect and you feel as if you are on top of the world? We don't get those moments often in real life, do we? Typically, the moment we are experiencing this feeling life has a way of crashing down around us. Right?

Can I tell you a story? It begins with Jesus, Savior to the world, Savior to me and you, who loved us enough to come down, living humbly, an everyday and ordinary life.

"In those days Jesus came from Nazareth in Galilee and was baptized in the Jordan by John. As soon as he came up out of the water, he saw the heavens being torn open and the Spirit descending on him like a dove. And a voice came from heaven: 'You are my beloved Son; with you I am well pleased.'" Mark 1:9-11 (CSB)

Jesus, the beloved Son of God, baptized in the Jordan by His cousin John. He comes up out of the water, the heavens are torn open, and we hear the voice of God. Wow! Other than crossing from this world to the next this is big.

Let's look deeper:

"Immediately the Spirit drove him into the wilderness. He was

in the wilderness forty days, being tempted by Satan. He was with the wild animals, and the angels were serving him." Mark 1:12-13 (CSB)

Here in Mark, we see Jesus raised from the water of the Jordan River and we hear the Voice of God. We see Him affirmed as His Beloved Son. The very next moment, He's driven into the wilderness. There, He spends forty days with Satan. The same low down, dirty-playing scoundrel, and evil adversary who chases us. Sound familiar?

A couple of weeks ago my Sweet Man spent Saturday doing mission work with our local church family. I spent the day watching Beth Moore's Captivated™ simulcast. When the simulcast ended I was on top of the world. High on Beth's teaching, praising at the top of my lungs, with only Sweet Lola to hear me, and holding pages of copious notes. The pinnacle of spirituality.

Until...

I fell off that mountaintop with a resounding thud. Truthfully, I leaped off, entering a nasty place. Grumped up, snarky, and discontent because Oprah's nutritionist/chef extraordinaire was not on-hand to prepare a tasty, nutritional meal for us. And while we are being honest, can I tell you? I felt discontentment with my home, my man, (who was Sweet in the prior paragraph), my life…

From a spiritual high to the lowest of lows! I quickly resembled the woman in *Proverbs 27:15,* rather than a godly woman who'd just spent her day under the teaching of Beth Moore!

"An endless dripping on a rainy day and nagging wife are alike."

OUCH!

I know the wilderness! I have been there. I **am** there, living daily with chronic illness and chronic pain. I also know a faithful God who tenderly meets me here. The same God who tended His only Beloved Son.

The reality of Jesus, experiencing the hard edges of life shined bright light into my reality. My own every day, ordinary life. Jesus, in His human form, experienced the same highs and lows of real life that we do today.

Humbling thought, hmm?

Journaling Prompt
How does it make you feel to know Jesus has experienced everything we have?

Will it change how you view your circumstances?

4 STIRRINGS

"Remain in me, and I in you." John 15:4 (CSB)

I have been unwinding a thread for months. It is as if I've pulled the first loose thread on a knitting project. I watch as it unravels in beautiful ways, tugging deeper on the garden of my heart.

It begins here: *"In the beginning there was the Word, and the Word was with God, and the Word was God." John 1:1 (CSB)*

The first small stirrings one needs to pay attention to.

I sat at the edge of a blueberry orchard, rows and rows of bushes heavy with fruit. Dew falls on my feet, as I watch my Sweet Man drop plump blueberries into his bucket, praise music pumping into my soul.

I ponder my heart searching areas where change needs to take place.

There was the barren fig tree Jesus cursed in Matthew, and the Parable of the Barren Fig Tree in Luke.

"Early in the morning, as he was returning to the city, he was hungry. Seeing a lone fig tree by the road, he went up to it and found nothing on it except leaves. And he said to it, 'May no fruit ever come from you again!' At once the fig tree withered." Matthew 21:18-22 (CSB)

"And he told this parable: 'A man had a fig tree that was planted in his vineyard. He came looking for fruit on it and found none. He told the vineyard worker, Listen, for three years I have come looking for fruit on this fig tree and haven't found any. Cut it down! Why should it even waste the soil?' But he replied to him, 'Sir, leave it this year also, until I dig around it

and fertilize it. Perhaps it will produce fruit next year, but if not, you can cut it down." Luke 13:6-9 (CSB)

For months, I have been drawn back to these two places in Scripture searching for what God is teaching me. Commentaries tell us the barren fig tree in Matthew represents Israel, even so, what is Jesus showing me?

I feel as if there's a connection, a theme, digging deep into my soul. I don't want a barren fig tree in the garden of my heart. I confess, I don't care to be pruned anymore. Isn't the wilderness enough? Isn't every imaginable life change enough? I have shed tears. I have done the work of walking through the valley. And, I have crossed the mountaintop. I have found, and seen, a faithful God I so badly want for you to find in your wilderness. I am determined to grow something good in this place. But, the pruning, not so much.

Pruning is never easy and often draws blood and tears.

We are a work in progress, there must always be pruning, tending, nourishing the soil in the garden of my heart. At the end of these are the things needed to grow and transform us, moving us closer to God, and making us more like Jesus.

Journaling Prompt

Is there something in your heart that needs tending today?

If so, what will you do to tend it?

5 TENDING MY GARDEN

I shared the work that God has been doing in my heart. A loose thread, unraveling and drawing me deeper into His Word.

The Parable of the Barren Fig Tree – Luke 13:6-9 (CSB)

"A man had a fig tree that was planted in his vineyard. He came looking for fruit on it and found none. He told the vineyard worker, 'Listen, for three years I have come looking for fruit on this fig tree and haven't found any. Cut it down! Why should it even waste the soil?'

"But he replied to him, 'Sir, leave it this year also, until I dig around it and fertilize it. Perhaps it will produce fruit next year, but if not, you can cut it down.'"

I am not a gardener by heart. I do not care to go anywhere near dirt, worms, bugs, and, yikes, a run-in with a slithering critter. According to my Sweet Man, this evokes, "the guttural cry of terror," (from Jaws). Nor, am I physically able, but, I do love the fruit of gardening. I enjoy beautiful blooms swaying in the breeze, hummingbirds spiraling in and sipping nectar, but the unpleasant truth is this: I don't want to do the work.

Digging into my soul, finding unwanted desires and thoughts is painful. Is it just me or do you grapple with this as well?

I read the words of Jesus, The Parable of the Barren Fig Tree pierces me deeply. I weep at the thought of standing in the same place, year after year – "Barren of Fruit."

In this parable, the vineyard worker has been given an extra year to work the soil around the tree. You and I have a merciful God, full of grace, who pursues and never gives up on us. Thank goodness! However, His grace and mercy do not give us a blank credit card to tuck away, waiting for a more convenient time to tend our souls.

Soul-tending has to begin today, now.

How do *I* do this?

· A time of lingering, praying His Word.

· Intentionality to go back day after day after day, even if, especially if, or when I may not want to. *PS: this is a good indicator I need soul work!*

· The determination not to give up.

· Cultivating a relationship with God.

· Pulling the weeds. That may mean giving up some things and taking up others.

· Sharing the faithfulness Jesus has shown to me so others will come to know Him.

When I cultivate, weed, and prune those dark, broken places in the garden of my soul, healthy growth takes place.

"Taste and see that the Lord is good." Psalm 34:8 (CSB)

Lingering in His Word gives me a taste of the life that is to come, eternity with Almighty God.

I love Him. I want Him. I want to bear fruit for His Kingdom.

"But the fruit of the Spirit is love, joy, peace, patience, kindness, goodness, faithfulness, gentleness, and self-control." Galatians 5:22 (CSB)

Journaling Prompt

What work needs to be done in the garden of your heart today?

What weeds do you need to pull?

Where does your garden need nurturing today?

6 KNOW HIS VOICE

The Shepherd leads with His voice.

Are we following His voice?

Do we know His voice?

Did you know the study of sheep is called Ovinology? I did not. I have become fascinated with sheep.

According to research, sheep can recognize faces of other sheep for up to two years. Sheep recognize the face and voice of their shepherd. They are social and have a need to see each other. Sheep have a strong instinct to follow the sheep in front of them, whether they are going towards danger or not.

"My sheep hear my voice, I know them, and they follow me."
John 10:26 (CSB)

Jesus is my Shepherd, if you are a believer, He is yours as well. As Believers, we are to follow His voice.

The sheep's instinct is to follow their leader, even when they are being led into danger. Over a cliff, or into a deep ravine, sheep will find themselves stuck until their shepherd comes searching for them.

I know this feeling very well. I have followed my own leading, the world's standards, and found myself in deep ravines. Tangled, ensnared by thorns and thistles. I have, and can, create a mess on my own. Like sheep, I need a good shepherd. I need guidance, wisdom, and nourishment. I need a reliable voice in my life. Sometimes I crave the knowledge of being seen by the Shepherd, and long for His reassurance.

How do I find that? Where do I find that? Where can you?

In His Word. By going to His Word, time and time again.

The answer is simple, yet, we are prone to ignore, make excuses, or break out in hives at the mere thought of commitment to spending time in His Word. It is much easier to do a drive-thru on Sunday mornings rather than do the work ourselves.

I know, I KNOW, my Sweet Man. I know his scent when he's near me, I recognize his voice from afar, the feel of his skin. We have been married thirty years, we've made an investment in time and intentionality in getting to know one another.

It is with the same investment and intentionality that we come to now the Shepherd's voice. If I want to know Jesus, The Good Shepherd, I must put in the work of learning His ways. His voice. His Word.

Make the investment.

If I want to know Jesus, know His voice, to know of His extravagant love for me, I have to go to the well of Living Water.

"Jesus answered, 'If you knew the gift of God and who is saying to you, 'Give me a drink,' you would ask him, and he would give you living water." John 4:10 (CSB)

Go to the well of Living Water. Get to know your Shepherd's voice. Invest the time. Make a commitment, be intentional, and be consistent.

His is the most important voice in your life. He will not lead you over a cliff or into a ravine. He will lead you to everlasting life.

Dearest Reader, if you do not know the Shepherd please do not hesitate to contact me by using the email on the author's page at the end of this book.

Journaling Prompt

How can you incorporate time in the Word in to your daily routine?

What changes do you need to make for this to happen?

7 HEARING OR TELLING?

Which one do I need to do?

"How then can they call on him they have not believed in? And how can they believe without hearing about him? And how can they hear without a preacher? And how can they preach unless they are sent? As it is written: How beautiful are the feet of those who bring good news." Romans 10:14-15 (CSB)

I am more prone to talk than listen. However, a certain personality test will tell you I am an introvert. I am. I thrive in my quiet space, I am hypersensitive to noise, very much liking routine and rhythm in my day. I am a slow processor, thoughtful, contemplative, and a bookworm. So happens I am a social introvert.

I am also a believer who is called to proclaim the Gospel and tell others of His faithfulness to me.

Once we know Christ, and have made Him Lord over our lives, we are commanded to become a teller of the Gospel.

I'm wondering where you sit on this? Are you someone who needs to hear the Gospel today? If so, please ask someone near you.

Hearers will become tellers!

If you are already a believer, you too are called to speak (a teller!), to tell of the wonderful things He has done for you. It is not always easy, is it?

When you find yourself in the midst of the wilderness, our first thought is not always of God's faithfulness. If we are honest, it is more likely, "Where are you God?"

Regardless of where we are or what we are, He sees us. He is still faithful and we should be telling our stories, and sharing His faithfulness to us.

Writing in my journal is where I have the sweetest time with God. His Word open, my journal, my favorite pen. It's where we communicate, where I pray, cry out, and give Him praise. It is also a resource I often refer back to when I am doubting where He is, who He is, or where He is working in my life.

When I am doubting, I often go to my shelves, searching out past journals. They are not fancy, poetic, or well-written, edited words. They are pages with coffee stains, tear stains, with ink smudged across the page. There are desperate pleas on the pages.

The stained pages, curled edges, tangible evidence of His faithfulness when I was faithless. Scriptures copied to the page, whisper into my soul. I can see His hand there, and there, and over there. Here, in the wilderness, where I am wrought with pain and heavy fatigue, I can see Him. And He sees me.

Second only to my Bible, I love my journals and combing back through them. They are my story, the story, I share when I tell of His faithfulness. Stories, that show His presence in the hard edges of life.

In Luke, chapter eight, Jesus drives the demons from a man. After his experience, there is nothing this man wants more than to be with Jesus. Jesus sends him home with these words:

"Go back to your home, and tell all that God has done for you." And off he went, proclaiming throughout the town how much Jesus had done for him. Luke 8:39 (CSB)

Jesus told the man what to do, "Go be a teller."

Which do you, do I, need to be doing today? Should we be hearing or telling?

It is a question every one of us needs to ask ourselves and honestly answer.

Journaling Prompt

Do you journal during your time alone with God?

If so, does it help you see God's faithfulness where you doubt His presence?

Are you encouraged when you look back through the pages of your journal and see God's presence?

8 DO YOU KNOW ME?

Seen in The Every Day

His Word is the breath in my lungs, the heartbeat of my soul. It is my survival guide.

There are punishing seasons in The Wilderness, P.O.T.S. rears its ugly head. By evening I am bent, folded in pain, barely making it to the bed. Collapsing, surrounded by thick brain fog, my bedtime routine a smoky haze.

On this particular night, in the midst of it all, simple, ordinary things become hard. I misplaced my favorite pair of earrings, my "signature" earrings.

Stumbling to my desk the next morning, I could not recall where I had laid the earrings. It is a small unimportant detail, missing earrings in the big picture of life. Random mass shootings, floods, hurricanes, cancer, devastation, and loss of life, and yet I was distracted by earrings. Yes, earrings, of all things.

My morning dialogue with the Lord was interrupted by this inconsequential thing circling my mind.

"I cry aloud to the Lord; I plead for mercy. I pour out my complaint before him; I reveal my trouble to him. Although my spirit is weak within me, you know my way." Psalm 142:1-3a (CSB)

I have spent hours and years, praying over weighty things, but this morning, a pair of earrings became a roadblock. Throwing my hands up in the air, disappointed and frustrated, "Lord, I want to find my earrings."

Can you relate? We get tangled up in the small things. One small thing stacks upon another until we cry out, "Lord, do You even see me?"

In the Gospel of John, chapter one, there was a man called Nathanael relaxing under a fig tree. His buddy, Philip, comes along and tells him they have found Jesus.

"The next day Jesus decided to leave for Galilee. He found Philip and told him, 'Follow me.'" Now Philip was from Bethsaida, the hometown of Andrew and Peter. Philip found Nathanael and told him, 'We have found the one Moses wrote about in the law (and so did the prophets): Jesus the son of Joseph, from Nazareth.'

'Come and see,' Philip answered.

Then Jesus saw Nathanael coming toward Him and said about him, 'Here truly is an Israelite in whom there is no deceit.'

'How do you know me?' Nathanael asked.

'Before Philip called you, when you were under the fig tree, I saw you,' Jesus answered." "I saw you," Jesus said, "when you were under the fig tree." John 1:43-48 (CSB)

The words bring me to my knees! Does it affect you as much as me?

Before moving forward, I want you to know I found my earrings tucked beneath the quilt. First one and then the other.

Here is the thing: He sees me. He sees you. In the everyday small and ordinary things. We long for the lit-up billboard that shows us we are seen. The accolades, the pat on the back, our platforms, ministries, and our agendas. The weighty unanswered prayers. We have to know this, believe this, cling to faith in the unseen. Cling to faith in the unanswered prayers, and we celebrate the small, everyday, ordinary things.

You are seen!

In a place filled with all manner of ugliness, celebrate that today!

"Lord, you have searched me and known me. You know when I sit down and when I stand up: you understand my thoughts from far away. You observe my travels and my rest; you are aware of all my ways. Before a word is on my tongue, you know all about it, Lord. You have encircled me; you have placed your hand on me. This wondrous knowledge is beyond me. It is lofty; I am unable to reach it." Psalm 139:1-6 (CSB)

Journaling Prompt

Where are you feeling unseen today?

Is there a chance you are missing God while searching for bigger things?

9 SLEEPING ON THE JOB

Praying in The Garden

"When he got up from prayer and came to the disciples, he found them sleeping, exhausted in their grief. 'Why are you sleeping?' he asked them. 'Get up and pray, so that you won't fall into temptation.'" Luke 22:45-46 (CSB)

We are living in a country, a world that is a heap of ugliness. We cry out, we do our best to make a difference in the cruelties happening around us. We are knee-deep in troubles.

Are we asleep on the job?

Some days I feel as if I am busy keeping myself above water, let alone doing the one pro-active thing I can standing exactly where I am: PRAY.

"Pray at all times in the Spirit with every prayer and request, and stay alert with all perseverance and intercession for all saints." Ephesians 6:18 (CSB)

I come up short in this area, easily distracted, most likely, you do as well.

"Then they came to a place named Gethsemane, and he told his disciples, 'Sit here while I pray.' He took, Peter, James, and John with him, and he began to be deeply distressed and troubled. He said to them, 'I am deeply grieved to the point of death. Remain here and stay awake.'" Mark 14:32-34 (CSB)

They were ordinary men who walked and ministered alongside Jesus. I am a bit encouraged that Peter, James, and John are not so different than me.

Jesus steps into the garden, falls to His knees and prays. Let's see what happens:

"Then he came and found them sleeping. He said to Peter, 'Simon, are you sleeping? Couldn't you stay awake one hour? Stay awake and pray so that you won't enter into temptation. The spirit is willing, but the flesh is weak.'" Mark 14:37-38 (CSB)

Jesus steps away from Peter, James, and John three times, each time He returned they were sleeping. I understand they have been through a lot, they know something big is about to happen, and they were tired.

Here is the thing, we serve a living, active God who never sleeps on the job. Never.

Why are we?

Is there something we need to change in our prayer lives? Prayer is less about us and more about God. Sacrificing time away from our phones, our laptops, Netflix, or anything that interferes with our prayer life. There is nothing, nothing, wrong with any of those things as long as they are not being used for evil or distracting from God.

Prayer is a conversation with God. A relationship. It is the place where we get on His agenda, not where we get Him on ours. Prayer is our most active tool against the evil in the world and in our own hearts. Prayer changes hearts and situations.

Prayer is holy communion with our Lord and Savior.

Are we sleeping on the job?

Am I? Are you?

Journaling Prompt

Is prayer a priority in your life?

Is prayer your go to in and for any circumstance?

What needs to change in your prayer life?

10 HEART MATTERS

Guard Your Heart

"Guard your heart above all else, for it is the source of life."
Proverbs 4:23 (CSB)

I want to freeze the moments, collect them as falling leaves. I counted the days as I gazed at a full moon through darkness. Four hundred ninety-six days have passed since that terrifying day.

There are days, and then, there are days. Days, where every detail is imprinted on your heart. The heat, the plants, the feel of grass beneath my feet as I ran in slow motion toward my Sweet Man, collapsing in pain. The sun bright above us, the taste of fear in my mouth. My own heart pounding in my chest, trembling from head to foot.

I sat in a hard, plastic chair, looking at the screen following the trail where blood passed through his heart. With a layman's eye, I saw the blood trapped, allowing only a minimum making it through, threatening his life.

"Guard your heart above all else, for it is the source of life."
Proverbs 4:23 (CSB)

Each time my eyes pass over this passage, I'm reminded again of the images I saw on the screen.

I'm reminded how everything passes through the heart, if not life stops.

What a picture, to watch blood make its way through the intricate maze of chambers in your heart.

Our spiritual heart is not so different, is it? Everything we look at, listen too, speak, read, take in, passes through our hearts.

We are willing to change our diets and lifestyles, cultivating a healthy and thriving heart. Our spiritual heart, we are willing to leave behind.

Why?

Everything we do flows through and from our hearts.

How do we keep a healthy spiritual heart?

1. Carefully monitor what passes through, such as what we watch, listen to, participate in, who we spend time with, and where we spend time.

2. Exercising. The heart is a muscle that loves to exercise therefore, we exercise our hearts by taking in, pondering, contemplating, and storing up the things of God.

Life-giving, Living Water is where we will find the treasure He has for us.

"God, create a clean heart for me and renew a steadfast spirit within me." Psalm 51:10 (CSB)

Renewing our heart in the ways of God is key to a healthy spiritual heart.

Journaling Prompt

What condition is your heart in today?

Is it blocked? If so, what do you need to change in your life?

Are you feeding your spiritual heart a steady diet of God's Word?

11 DESPERATE FOR JESUS

"He entered Jericho and was passing through. There was a man named Zacchaeus who was a chief tax collector, and he was rich. He was trying to see who Jesus was, but he was not able to because of the crowd, since he was a short man. So running ahead, he climbed up a sycamore tree to see Jesus, since he was about to pass that way." Luke 19:1-4 (CSB)

The delightful gift reaped from The Wilderness has been learning to lean into His quiet whispers, lingering with Him.

The story of Zacchaeus speaks to me on many levels. First off, Zacchaeus is short, "a wee little man," the children's song says. I am a full fifty-nine and a quarter inches, with hair product. I can relate to looking over heads. Trying to get the attention of the person I am seeking is frustrating!

Our small friend was desperate to see Jesus. Desperate enough to clamor up a tree causing a scene.

"When Jesus came to the place, he looked up and said to him, 'Zacchaeus, hurry and come down because today it is necessary for me to stay at your house.' so he quickly came down and welcomed him joyfully." Luke 19:5-6 (CSB)

Are we as desperate as Zacchaeus, going to the extreme of clamoring up a tree, calling out His name?

Or, are we simply too busy, distracted, or just not interested in going to Him first. Crying out, "Jesus, over here! I need you."

We need Him so, He is the Sustainer of all life, the Peace that passes all understanding, our intercessor, standing in the gap for us. Standing before God, pleading on our behalf.

Often, it is easier to call a friend or seek social media, anything to avoid crying out to Jesus. To call out to Him is to face our inadequacies, admitting weakness, or giving up our need for control. It exposes our sin and brokenness.

Grace upon grace washes over our inadequacies. Grace upon grace, unfolding grace. His mercy covers our sin and brokenness, His mercies are new every morning.

My desperation and need drive me toward Him, not away from Him.

To be desperate for Him is to find Him.

Zacchaeus wanted more than just seeing Jesus. He realized there was more to be had. He realized salvation could be his. Zacchaeus wanted it all.

"Who is this coming up from the wilderness leaning on the one she loves?" Song of Solomon 8:5 (CSB)

Journaling Prompt
What keeps you from crying out to God?

Do you turn to something or someone else first? If so, why?

How does that make you feel?

12 GRACE IN HOLLOW PLACES

Grace fills our cavernous, hollowed out places. We split our brittle hearts wide and grace falls in.

Have you ever spoken the Word out loud?

I am not thinking of reading it before a group of people. Have you spoken the Word out loud, between you and the Lord, and maybe your dog or cat?

Most evenings I spend time at my desk, reflecting on my day, reading Scripture, and writing in my journal. I record moments that spoke to me, moments I do not want to forget.

Squinty-eyed, fatigue rolling over me, last evening I read John, chapter twenty, out loud. In my tiredness, I wanted, needed to be moved by God.

Every word edged with desperation. He delivered and I cried ugly tears.

"I called to the Lord in my distress, and I cried to my God for help. From his temple he heard my voice, and my cry to him reached his ears." Psalms 18:6 (CSB)

I have read through John's gospel many times but this time, I noticed something I have never noticed before.

"On the first day of the week Mary Magdalene came to the tomb early, while it was still dark. She saw that the stone had been removed from the tomb. So she went running to Simon Peter and to the other disciple, the one Jesus loved, and said to them, 'They've taken the Lord out of the tomb, and we don't know where they've put Him!'

At that, Peter and the other disciple went out, heading for the tomb. The two were running together, but the other disciple outran Peter and got to the tomb first. Stooping down, he saw the linen clothes lying there but he did not go in. Then, following him, Simon Peter also came. He entered the tomb and saw the linen cloths lying there.

The wrapping that had been on His head was not lying with the linen cloths BUT was FOLDED up in a separate place by itself. (verse 7b-emphasis mine)

The other disciple, who had reached the tomb first, then also went in, saw and believed." John 20:1-8 (CSB)

Did you notice? The wrapping from His head was not with the other linen cloths but was folded up in a separate place by itself.

Standing at the empty tomb, my gaze scanning the scene, I see the pile of linen cloths. Upon searching deeper, in another place lies the wrapping from His head, FOLDED! I see a Savior with a tender heart, quietly folding the cloth, taking time to place it just so, for me. For us. Grace upon grace unfolds in hollow places deep in my heart. I feel His tenderness wrap around me, His grace rain over me. I am undone.

I wonder if the disciples, in their shock, missed that one small detail? We don't know, nothing is mentioned one way or the other. In my desperation to hear His voice, he brought this detail to life for me, personally.

His Word is alive and active!

I find more than grace in the folded linen. I see a promise, the promise that he is not finished. He is not finished with me or with you, He is coming back!

I pray that I will never stop being surprised by Him!

Journaling Prompt

Has he surprised you lately?

In what way and how did it make you feel?

13 BROKEN BEFORE THE CRY

Why must we be broken before we cry out?

Often, we speak of the Israelites in the Bible as stiff-necked and stubborn. I am not much different from the Israelites. I am just as stubborn, set in my ways, without much tolerance to veering outside of my lane, and flat out stubborn as a mule. Just ask my Sweet Man.

"He broke their spirits with hard labor, they stumbled, and there was no one to help. Then they cried out to the Lord in their trouble; and he saved them from their distress." Psalms 107:12-13

I can relate to being broken before the cry, can you? When life is without storms, I happily skip along, placing God on the back burner. It's not until I stumble before I realize my need.

Sound familiar?

It is when I find myself in the midst of a storm, broken shards scattered at my feet, I cry out for God. Stumbling, reaching for the hand reaching for me. Why did I not cry out sooner?

And, shouldn't I be crying out in the good as well? Crying out in praise and worship?

Praising and worshiping in the good and the bad? Why am I so arrogant as to wait until I'm broken before I cry out to Him?

I am prideful. We are prideful and fickle people who control and manipulate our way out of needing God. Living from a place of self-reliance. We cover our weaknesses, put masks on our faces, tweet the good stuff, filter our Instagram feed, and stage the pictures. Sound familiar?

Need is a weakness we cover.

"My grace is sufficient for you, for my power is made strong in weakness." 2 Corinthians 12:9 (CSB)

We were created to need. Created to need a loving God who is waiting on us to cry out to Him. We are not meant to do life without Him, nor do I want to.

Life without God is not worth living.

And I do not want it. I want God. I want God in the good, the hard, and the broken. I want His strength and grace in my weakness.

Journaling Prompt

Do you find you wait until the storms before you cry out to God?

Are you praising and worshiping Him in the good and the broken?

14 SEEKING AND SEARCHING

Are we seeking Him in our brokenness, our wilderness places, or are we sweeping broken shards to the darkest corners of our souls?

"You will seek me and find me when you search for me with all your heart." Jeremiah 29:13 (CSB)

We begin in a familiar place, a Scripture most of us memorized as a young child, easily plucked from the dark recesses of my mind. Tucked away from long ago days with flannel boards and small wooden chairs.

I went word searching, looking for the original meanings and connotations.

· Seek: "To search out (by any method, specifically in worship or prayer); by implication, to strive after." Bible Hub's Lexicon

· Search: "to tread or frequent; usually to follow (for pursuit or search); by implication, to seek or ask; specifically, to worship."

· Heart: "The heart (as the most interior organ.)"

We connect together words seek, search, and heart, mix them with the word ALL: "The whole of any, whatever, beyond all doubt. The whole quantity or amount, everything." (from Dictionary.com)

Stitched together, Jeremiah 29:13 becomes more than a memory verse on a flannel board, it is the heartbeat of who we are. Deep in our souls, it is everything we were created for.

Seeking, searching, never giving up, in spite of our wilderness places.

In our wilderness places. The wilderness is where you need Him most. He becomes, He is the breath in our lungs, the strength for your next step.

Do we seek Him with our entire being, while the pieces of our broken heart lay in shards, shattered around us? Are we more prone to sweep up our brokenness to the darkest corners, deep in our souls, giving up on seeking?

A.W. Tozer from his book, *The Root of the Righteous* says this:

"The Christian is strong or weak depending upon how closely he has cultivated the knowledge of God."

Strength is cultivated with knowledge of God.

Deep roots grow when we seek and search The Word. He is there, on the pages. He is in gentle breezes, downy hair on a baby's head. The butterfly sitting up on the last vestiges of blooms.

He is in the storm, the thunder, and lightening. He is in the crashing waves.

He is in the big, in the small, the great, the ordinary, and the mundane.

He is in the good and the bad.

Journaling Prompt

Are we seeking Him in every area of our lives?

Are we searching, even when we do not want to find Him?

15 DO YOUR WORK AND STOP COMPARING

Answer your calling, serve from your sweet spot and stop looking over your shoulder, comparing your ministry to someone else.

Serve where you are planted.

"If I want him to remain until I come," Jesus answered, "what is that to you? As for you, follow me." John 21:22 (CSB)

These words come from a place of deep work in my own heart. He is ever pruning me, planting His Word deeper into my heart. It is sometimes painful. Growing pains typically are.

Theodore Roosevelt said this: "Comparison is the thief of all joy."

As women, comparison is our biggest enemy. Social media has given us a way to present our best selves and with it, the need to scroll through the feed checking to see if we made the cut. Right?

In John's last chapter we see a picture of Peter doing the same. John 21:15-19 is a picture of Peter's restoration after his denial of Christ, three times. Side note: How often do I deny Him? Ouch! One would Think restoration would be enough. But, it is not. Comparison moves Peter to take his eyes off Jesus looking over his shoulder, worrying about the other guy.

"So Peter turned around and saw the disciple Jesus loved following them, the one who had leaned back against Jesus at the supper and asked, 'Lord, who is the one that's going to betray

you?' When Peter saw him, he said to Jesus, 'Lord, what about him?' 'If I want him to remain until I come,' Jesus answered, 'what is that to you? As for you, follow me.'" John 21:20-22 (CSB)

Jesus restores Peter after his betrayal, and he wants to know about this other fellow. "What about him?"

Peter, one of many, who I most want to have coffee and long conversations with; he's not much different than you or me. Jesus has just handed him his ministry, his walking orders.

· Feed my lambs.

· Do you love me?

· Feed my sheep.

· You will die for me.

· Follow me.

Straight up, no questions asked, Jesus lays one of the most significant ministries we see in the New Testament into Peter's hands. Immediately, Peter looks over his shoulder, and says, "What about him?"

Sound familiar?

Comparison robs us of joy, taints our ministry, questions our motives, and causes heartache to yourself and possibly others.

Comparison opens a gap for dissension and bitterness to grow.

What follows in this dialogue between Jesus and Peter is painful, yet straightforward. "What is that to you? As for you, follow me."

With a posture of surrendered obedience, your service, your ministry is yours. It is the most important thing, regardless of what it is. It does not matter one skinny minute, what mine may be, or what so and so with the perfect Instagram feed and the large following is doing either.

What matters is that I, that you, are following Jesus and serving Him with a heart of surrendered obedience and doing the next thing.

How do we do this?

Start here:

- Become a student of His Word.

- Find a Godly mentor.

- Grow in the life and manner of prayer.

- Seek Godly counsel.

- Listen. *"Be still and know that I am God." Psalm 46:10 (NIV)*

- Have a posture of surrendered obedience.

Comparison moves Peter to take his eyes off Jesus. Comparison drives us to take our eyes off Jesus and chase perfection.

I must do my work and you must do your work and we must stop comparing.

Journaling Prompt

Where do you struggle most with comparison?

How can you learn to be content in your lane, not looking around at the other person?

16 THE COST OF IDOLATRY

Idolatry leads to secrecy, self-destruction, temporary fulfillment, jealousy, exposure, and spiritual death.

Today's words are perhaps the hardest words to write as I sweep my own idols out of the closet for you to see. We like our idols hidden and shrouded in secrecy.

Let's peek at the idolatry going on in Ezekiel, Chapter 8:

"The Lord said to me, 'Son of man, look toward the north.' I looked to the north, and there was this offensive statue north of the Alter Gate, at the entrance. He said to me, 'Son of man, do you see what they are doing here-more detestable acts that the house of Israel is committing-so that I must depart from my sanctuary? You will see even more detestable acts.'

Then he brought me to the entrance of the court, and when I looked there was a hole in the wall. He said to me, 'Son of man, dig through the wall.' So I dug through the wall and discovered a doorway. He said to me, 'Go in and see the detestable, wicked acts they are committing here.'" Ezekiel 8:8-9 (CSB)

God gives Ezekiel a vision, the first thing he sees in the temple is an idol. According to Warren W. Wiersbe's commentary, the idol is called, *"The image of jealousy, because idolatry provokes the Lord who is jealous of His people."*

In this passage of Scripture, we get a glimpse of open idolatry and hidden idols. Ezekiel, instructed to look north, sees an offensive statue north of the Alter Gate, at the entrance. Ezekiel is taken deeper in his vision, told by God to dig through a wall, go in and see the detestable, wicked acts being committed. The farther

Ezekiel is taken in, the more detestable the wickedness becomes, sickening God. God responds with wrath.

What follows, are the saddest words I can imagine hearing from God.

"Therefore I will respond with wrath. I will not show pity or spare them. Though they call loudly in my hearing, I WILL NOT LISTEN TO THEM." Ezekiel 8:18 (CSB) (emphasis mine)

My first thought, "I'm thankful I am nothing like these people."

Only, I am. I also prefer keeping my idols hidden or covered up. Hidden, my idolatry goes undetected. I can almost pretend it doesn't exist. Do you experience the same?

I have not driven in almost five years. Impulse trips to Target or Marshall's, while sipping on the sweet nectar of Starbucks, are no longer a part of my days. However, I can scroll through my laptop, finding a plethora of shopping sites to peruse. Amazon, and other sites, bring me instant gratification without leaving home. One push of a button and I can order anything I want.

For someone who is mostly home-bound, that is more temptation than I can stand. On top of that, books are my love language. Between social media, advertisements, and my own imagined need to have books, this has become an idol. An idol I struggle to kick from my heart. A temptation clamoring for my attention.

Making matters worse, I am prone to seal my lips, not letting my Sweet Man know I have ordered anything. Not only is he the spiritual head of our home, he keeps our budget and finances in order. I should be speaking to him before I purchase, rather than hoping the big brown truck shows up while he is out! It never plays out that way, and I am forced to come clean. These are hard truths.

I have built an idol, my own golden calf, from the confines of my home, justifying it with my illness.

Concealing it from my Sweet Man, my idols become a source of contention. My idolatry becomes a source of secrecy, denial, over spending, temporary fulfillment, exposure, and disappointment on my Sweet Man's face. Worse, it is sin, and sin separates me from God.

I carry the guilt, the heavy weight of sin, that I must continually work to rid myself of. If not, there is the cost of spiritual death. OUCH!

"The sorrows of those who take another god for themselves will multiply.' Psalms 18:4a (CSB)

Do not despair, we are a continual work in progress. The key is to continue taking our idols before the Throne of Grace and mercy, destroying them.

Journaling Prompt

Can you identify any idols in your heart?

If so, what do you plan to do with them?

What boundaries need to be put in place to protect you in this area of your life?

17 CHARACTERISTICS OF SPIRITUAL GROWTH

"Complacency is a deadly foe of all spiritual growth." A.W. Tozer

My growing up days I spent longing for growth. I wanted to grow a bit taller. Grow into a bigger clothing size. Grow to be seen and chosen for the kickball team, even though I hated kickball.

These days I cry out for spiritual growth. I found Him in the wilderness, fell in love with Him on the mountaintop. I long to go deeper, to grow in His knowledge and wisdom. To decrease as He increases.

Let's look at the characteristics of spiritual growth. What does it look like? What does it take?

We will start with Paul's prayer for spiritual growth.

"For this reason also, since the day we heard this, we haven't stopped praying for you. We are asking that you may be filled with knowledge of his will in all wisdom and spiritual understanding, so that you may walk worthy of the Lord, fully pleasing to him: bearing fruit in every good work and growing in the knowledge of God, being strengthened with all power, according to his glorious might, so that you may have great endurance and patience, joyfully giving thanks to the Father, who has enabled you to share in the saints' inheritance in the light. He has rescued us from the domain of darkness and transferred us into the Kingdom of the Son he loves. In him we have redemption, the forgiveness of sins." Colossians 1: 9-14 (CSB)

Characteristics of Spiritual Growth:

- Filled With the Knowledge of His Will

Where do we find His will? In His Word, and not by sampling it, but digging deep in the layers of wisdom and life. This takes a commitment of time in His Word. Making time daily to spend with the Lord. It also requires consistency. Consistent with time, effort, reading, studying, and seeking Godly counsel to answer your questions.

James 1:5 (CSB) says this, "Now if any of you lacks wisdom, he should ask God-gives to all generously and ungrudgingly-and it will be given to him."

- Walk Worthy of The Lord

How do we walk worthy of the Lord? By walking in surrendered obedience to His will and not our own. Living in a way that does not bring shame to Him. Walking with the power of the Holy Spirit, which lives in us. Pleasing Him in all that we do. He must increase as we decrease. Walking worthy is to die to self, take up His cross and follow Him. At all costs.

"He must increase, but I must decrease." John 3:30 (CSB)

"Then he said to them all. 'If anyone wants to follow after me, let him deny himself, take up his cross daily and follow me." Luke 9:23 (CSB)

- Bear Fruit

Bearing fruit requires deep roots planted in fertile soil. Tending the soil of your heart daily. Pruning the bad, nourishing the good. Bearing fruit is cultivating love, joy, peace, patience, kindness, goodness, faithfulness, gentleness, and self-control. No matter our circumstances, in spite of our circumstances.

"But the fruit of the Spirit is love, joy, peace, patience, kindness, goodness, faithfulness, gentleness, and self-control. The law is not against such things." Galatians 5:22 (CSB)

- Growth in Knowledge

Growth in knowledge of Him is a daily commitment. A daily sacrificing oneself to the cross. Continually seeking Him in ALL things.

"For this very reason, make every effort to supplement your faith with goodness, goodness with knowledge, knowledge with self-control, self-control with endurance, endurance with godliness, with brotherly affection with love. For if you possess these qualities in increasing measure, they, will keep you from being useless or unfruitful in the knowledge of our Lord Jesus Christ." 2 Peter 1:5-8 (CSB)

Just as an athlete builds endurance, spiritual growth also requires building endurance; through endurance and patience we learn to live joyfully.

Spiritual growth is active and lively, complacency leads to spiritual death.

Journaling Prompt:

Are you using your best, your only, defense: The Word of God?

Do you have consistent time in The Word?

If not, what do you need to change in your life to have consistent time in The Word?

18 FIGHTING FOR YOUR SOUL

Preparing for battle means gathering the right weapons of defense.

Tempted by Satan, Jesus Himself pointed the way for us in the wilderness. We learn the best weapons of defense through the Son of God.

"Then Jesus was led up by the Spirit into the wilderness to be tempted by the devil. After he had fasted forty days and forty nights, he was hungry. Then the tempter approached him and said, 'If you are the Son of God tell these stones to become bread.'

He answered, 'It is written: Man must not live on bread alone but on every word that comes from the mouth of God.'

Then the devil took him to the holy city, had him stand on the pinnacle of the temple, and said to him, 'If you are the Son of God, throw yourself down. For it is written: He will give his angels orders concerning you, and they will support you with their hands so that you will not strike your foot against a stone.'

Jesus told him, 'If it is also written: Do not test the Lord your God.'

Again, the devil took him to a very high mountain and showed him all the kingdoms of the world and their splendor. And he said to him, 'I will give you all these things if you will fall down and worship me.'

Then Jesus told him, 'Go away, Satan! For it is written: Worship the Lord your God, and serve only him.'

Then the devil left him, and angels came and began to serve him." Matthew 4:1-11 (CSB)

Jesus had been in the wilderness forty days and forty nights, fasting and praying. I suspect Jesus was strengthened through this time of prayer with His Father while at the same time weakened by forty days and nights without food.

The first thing I notice is Satan knew where to find Jesus, just as he knows where to find us. I don't see the enemy quietly slithering into the wilderness. Instead, he boldly steps through the door of Jesus' weakness. In the same manner, he sashays boldly into our weakest places.

The enemy boldly walks through our doors with the intent to destroy our souls.

Jesus had His weapons in place, ready to defend Himself. Jesus used words as His weapon, not just any words, but the Word of God. His defense, quoting the Word of God.

Are we in a position to defend ourselves? Do we hold in our hand the weapons we need to fight an unseen enemy?

How we can we fight if we are not familiar with the weapons? How can we fight if we do not know His Word? Is the weapon we need collecting dust on a shelf? We find ourselves empty-handed and soul-weary, famished and starving.

"Look, the days are coming-this is the declaration of the Lord God-when I will send a famine through the land: not a famine of bread or a thirst for water, but of hearing the words of the Lord." Amos 8:11 (CSB)

In our hunger, we are weak. Weakened to the point of missing our adversary as he sets up housekeeping in our hearts. He sets up housekeeping in our homes, marriages, finances, children, our desires, and every area of our lives.

When we are in His Word, we have the weapons needed to fight, just as Jesus had what he needed.

"The instruction of the Lord is perfect, renewing one's life; the testimony of the Lord is trustworthy, making the inexperienced wise." Psalm 19:7 (CSB)

"So my word that comes from my mouth will not return to me empty, but it will accomplish what I please and will prosper in what I send it to do." Isaiah 55:11 (CSB)

"Take the helmet of salvation and the sword of the Spirit-which is the WORD OF GOD." Ephesians 7:17 (CSB)

Your sword, your weapon is the Word of God. Take it up, learn it, pray it, speak it. It is your defense.

Preparing for battle means gathering the right weapon of defense.

Fighting for our souls is to fight for our lives.

Journaling Prompt

Are you using your best, your only, defense: The Word of God?

Does this include scripture memorization?

With His Word do you feel stronger when the Adversary comes against you?

19 FINDING LIFE IN THE VALLEY OF DRY BONES

I need life breathed into dry bones. Life breathed into dry and dusty places. I cannot exist in The Wilderness as dry bones. I will not live where there is no laughter, joy, peace, or life.

I live in The Wilderness of chronic illness, an illness that does not have a cure. I live with dry and brittle bones, aching every moment of my days and nights.

I do not care to spend my days in grim severity or bitterness. I choose to live them fully, stewarding well the story God has given me. Do I believe I am a superhero? No! Am I more spiritual than the next person? No. I am broken and needy, searching for beauty with every part of my being. Searching for God in the moments of my days.

I can seek Him and find Him, or I can give up. I am not giving up. I am choosing to live well the story God has given me to carry.

"The hand of the Lord was on me, and he brought me out by his Spirit and set me down in the middle of the valley; it was full of bones. He led me all around them. There were a great many of them on the surface of the valley, and they were very dry. Then he said to me, 'Son of man, can these bones live?'

I replied, 'Lord God, only you know.'" Ezekiel 37:1-3 (CSB)

According to commentaries, the dry bones represent the whole Jewish nation. However, the point of this event is to affirm, with God all things are possible. The bodies lacked life. What brings life?

"Prophesy concerning these and say to them: Dry bones, hear the word of the Lord! This is what the Lord God says to these bones: I will cause breath to enter you, and you will live." Ezekiel 37:4-5

His breath. His breath brings life.

"When Ezekiel spoke the living word of God, the breath from God entered the dead bodies and they lived and stood to their feet." Warren W. Wiersbe-Be Reverent: Bowing Before Our Awesome God

"I will put tendons on you, make flesh grow on you, and cover you with skin. I will put breath in you so that you come to life. Then you will know that I am the Lord." Ezekiel 37:6 (CSB)

God instructs Ezekiel to continue prophesying, and as Ezekiel obeys, there is a rattling sound as the bones come together. I get chill bumps every time I read these words. I imagine my rattling bones, the popping and cracking that comes with movement. I want the breath of God deep in my soul, deep in my bones. I desire life. I choose life. I accept His breath, His Spirit living in me.

God breathed life into Adam; Adam, formed by dust, brought to life by the breath of God. (from Genesis 2:7)

"The Spirit of God has made me, and the breath of the Almighty gives me life." Job 33:4 (CSB)

"The heavens were made by the word of the Lord, and all the stars, by the breath of his mouth." Psalms 33:6 (CSB)

Just as God breathes life into man, He breathes the stars into place. He breathes life into our dry and dusty places. Our brokenness. He gives life in the unholy hard.

"The fellowship of God is delightful beyond all telling." A.W. Tozer – The Root of the Righteous

The fellowship of God is my delight, my heart's desire. I cannot move through the wilderness any other way.

Wherever you may be today, I pray you turn to Him for life. I pray you open your heart and your broken places to His breath.

Journaling Prompt

Are you living in the Valley of Dry Bones?

What needs to happen to change that?

20 CLOTHED IN CHRIST

What are we wearing?

"For those of you who were baptized into Christ have been clothed with Christ." Galatians 3:27 (CSB)

I have been searching my heart, soul-scaping I call it. Looking for unruly places that need pruning. I ran across Galatians 3:27 a couple of weeks ago. It made enough noise to warrant a post-it note over my words.

"For those of you who were baptized into Christ have been clothed with Christ." Galatians 3:27 (CSB)

With the winter preparations, I pondered my spiritual clothing. "Am I clothed in Christ?" Yes, I have surrendered my life to Christ, but am I clothed in Him? Once we have been baptized and transformed, doesn't that mean we should appear differently than the world?

Yes, it does.

I did some digging and learned that to be clothed in Christ is a picture of sinking into a garment.

"To be clothed is to invest in; clothing-literally or figuratively-array, clothe with, to spend or endow with some gift, quality or faculty." (biblehub.com/lexicon)

How does this play out in my life? What changes must I make?

What are the characteristics of being clothed with Christ?

"Therefore, as God's chosen ones, holy and dearly loved, put on compassion, kindness, humility, gentleness, and patience, bearing

with one another and forgiving one another if anyone has a grievance against one another. Just as the Lord has forgiven you, so you are also to forgive. Above all, put on love, which is the perfect bond of unity." Colossians 3:12-14 (CSB)

Compassion *"For the Lord is good to everyone; his compassion rests on all he has made." Psalms 145:9 (CSB)*

Kindness *"But when the kindness of God our Savior and his love for mankind appeared, he saved us – not by works of righteousness that we had done, but according to his mercy." Titus 3:4-5a (CSB)*

Humility *"When arrogance comes, disgrace follows, but with humility comes wisdom." Proverbs 11:2 (CSB)*

Gentleness *"Remind them to submit to rulers and authorities, to obey, to be ready for every good work, to slander no one, to avoid fighting, and to be kind, always showing gentleness to all people." Titus 3:1-2*

Patience *"A person's insight gives him patience and his virtue is to overlook an offense." Proverbs 19:11 (CSB)*

"Preach the word; be ready in season and out of season; rebuke, correct, and encourage with great patience and teaching." 2 Timothy 4:2 (CSB)

Forgiving *"For if you forgive others their offenses, your heavenly Father will forgive you as well. But if you don't forgive others, your Father will not forgive your offenses." Matthew 6:14-15 (CSB)*

Love *"Love is patient, love is kind. Love does not envy, is not boastful, is not arrogant, is not rude, is not self-seeking, is not irritable, and does not keep a record of wrongs." 1 Corinthians 13:4-5 (CSB)*

"Above all, maintain constant love for one another, since love covers a multitude of sins." 1 Peter 4:8 (CSB)

Life in Christ is transforming, or at least it should be. Know that I am talking to myself here! If we have grown up in the Church, we know the "thou shall not's." Somewhere in the midst is grace that washes over us and clothes us in beauty.

We simply need to put on the "right things."

Beauty shines into the broken edges of our lives.

We have to be intentional in choosing our spiritual clothing. What we wear, how we wear it, will either draw others to His saving grace or send them running away!

Journaling Prompts

Does your "spiritual clothing" resemble these characteristics?

What needs to be added or taken away from your spiritual wardrobe?

21 PRIDE

Pride empties the soul, inflates egos, leaves us restless, and robs us of integrity.

Pride, a subject that pokes holes in every part of my being. I wish I could tell you differently, wish it did not have a strangle hold on me.

It is one of my biggest struggles. When I follow the thread of pride in my heart, it leaks and spreads into every area of my life.

My pride lies at the root of every other weakness in my life. I.Know.That. Pride is like stepping into an angry mound of fire ants. Before I know what is happening, it is not one ant stinging, but droves of them. One ant follows another and another. Before you know what is happening they spread into your clothing, socks, shoes, and other crevices they might find to cause misery and pain.

I detest the little pests, and yet, I am willing to tolerate my pride. Some days going so far as to embrace it.

I cannot begin to list every Scripture in the Word concerning pride. There are many. I want to share a small sampling with you.

"Though the Lord is exalted, he takes note of the humble; but he knows the haughty from a distance." Psalms 138:6 (CSB)

"When arrogance comes, disgrace follows, but with humility comes wisdom." Proverbs 11:2 (CSB)

"Everyone with a proud heart is detestable to the Lord; be assured, he will not go unpunished." Proverbs 16:5 (CSB)

"A person's pride will humble him, but a humble spirit will gain honor." Proverbs 29:23 (CSB)

Lastly, Habakkuk 2:4 in first the CSB translation, followed by Eugene Peterson's, The Message.

"Look, his ego is inflated; he is without integrity. But the righteous one will live by his faith."

"Look at that man, bloated by self-importance - full of himself but soul-empty. But the person in right standing before God through loyal and steady believing is fully alive, really alive."

Pride leaves us soul-empty.

With pride, we are:

- Soul-empty
- Bloated by self-importance
- Haughty
- Arrogant
- Without integrity

When we demolish pride, we are:

- Loyal
- Steady
- In right standing with God
- Humble
- Fully alive
- Faithful and living righteously

This side of my life I will never entirely eradicate pride. However, I am intentional to shut it down before it runs too far out of control. I am diligent in capturing my prideful thoughts, taking them captive to His Word. I can only pray that I will decrease as He increases. Grace. More Grace, upon grace, from a loving, merciful God.

"Since the weapons of our warfare are not of the flesh, but are powerful through God for the demolition of strongholds. We demolish arguments and every proud thing that is raised up against the knowledge of God, and we take every thought captive to obey Christ." 2 Corinthians 10:4-5 (CSB)

Journaling Prompt

Is pride a struggle for you?

What boundaries and tools can you use to demolish the stronghold of pride?

22 CALM IN THE STORM

My storm did not come with either wind or rain. I was stranded in The Wilderness, living in the midst of the unknown, fading away with each passing day.

Survival felt beyond my reach.

I am not surprised on this day as I chose to write about my storm, the wind fiercely blows, rattling windows. Rain beats a steady rhythm on the roof. Cozy darkness surrounds me. I am no longer afraid; I found calm in the midst of my storm.

Today, I want to share a small sampling of my story with you.

"My storm did not come with either wind or rain. I was stranded in The Wilderness, living in the midst of the unknown, fading away with each passing day. Survival felt beyond my reach."

Survival in the wilderness often feels beyond our reach.

An unexpected whirlwind blew over my life, stripping me of what was. I ignored the signs. Dark clouds hovered near, and I chose not to see them. I wanted to believe life as I knew it would not fall away.

When you feel the unholy hard coming your way, you choose to ignore it, wish to believe you are invincible and will not be affected by such things. If you live long enough, you will be knocked over at least once by a raging storm.

James tells us the same.

"Consider it a great joy, my brothers and sisters, whenever you experience various trials, because you know that the testing of your faith produces endurance. And let endurance have its full effect, so that you may be mature and complete, lacking nothing." James 1:2-4 (CSB)

Pieces of my life, cut away, left me flailing about in my doctor's words, "No cure, only managing." In a matter of time, everything familiar to me was gone. My job, driving, running, leaving our home, dressing myself, standing, any semblance of independence. One by one they departed without asking permission.

Stripped of self-reliance, led to the wilderness in the midst of a raging storm. The first of my hard days, just finding the strength to fight was beyond my grasp.

Stretching my fingertips, turning pages, I read of another storm.

"As he got into the boat, his disciples followed him. Suddenly, a violent storm arose on the sea, so that the boat was being swamped by the waves – but Jesus kept sleeping. So the disciples came and woke him up, saying, 'Lord, save us! We're going to die!'

He said to them, 'Why are you afraid, you of little faith?' Then he got up and rebuked the winds and the sea and there was a great calm." Matthew 8:23-26 (CSB)

I was terrified! I had come to a place where any illusion of control was gone, left with choosing faith or choosing a life of fear, giving up and giving in. There was my Sweet Man with his furrowed brow, the precious faces of my grandchildren and children watching me. My Soul Sister, pushing and prodding, often dragging me forward, refusing to let me give up.

Moving forward meant leaning on a strength I did not have, could not get, nor possess on my own.

I chose the boat with Jesus in it. I fell into His embrace in the wilderness. I needed calm in the storm. When I tell you this, likely you may think I am stretching the truth. I.Am.Not.

In the midst of the storm, I found calm. I found peace that passes all understanding. Peace, I did not, could not, begin to understand. Supernatural peace.

My unraveling became the sweetest time with the Lord. In the midst of the unholy hard, I stepped into the Wilderness, my hand in His, and I walked on the mountaintop, the unholy hard became a holy place.

I want so badly to take your beautiful face in my hands and tell you, "You too can have the same." Is it easy? No, it is just as James says, a trial. Pain is deep and relentless and still, there is calm. There is joy. If you do not get one thing from this story, I implore you to get this.

There is more than surviving; there is thriving in The Wilderness.

You can have the same. You too can have Jesus. You are His beloved. He longs to be yours. He is in the midst of our storms, calming, protecting, holding. We have to choose to believe.

Journaling Prompt

Are you currently in a storm?

If so, are you merely surviving or thriving?

23 SINK OR SWIM: JUMPING OVERBOARD

We waffle between staying in the boat or jumping overboard. Choosing to step out of the boat with Jesus, I sink.

I shared this with you in our last installment:

"I chose the boat with Jesus in it. I fell into His embrace in the wilderness. I needed calm in the storm."

That is where I am today, in the boat with Jesus. Walking, sometimes dancing, sometimes being carried through the wilderness.

If you have not chosen Jesus, my heart longs to share a time when I jumped out of the boat. Angry with God, I turned away from Him. I was willing to lose it all and sink in a life without Jesus. I chose to descend into a pit of hell.

I cannot swim!

We did not live near water, nor was there a public pool in my growing up years. In my adult years, I took swimming lessons, on the chance I might need to jump in and save my children. I failed all attempts at learning to swim. I defied all logic and sank; the swimming instructor gently advised me to quit trying. I did.

Jumping out of my metaphorical, spiritual boat did not go any better. It was ugly and came close to costing me everything.

Without Jesus, we will sink. There are no protective boundaries in place. No rock to stand on when the swells wash over you, tugging you under water. There is no breath in your lungs, no life in your days.

There is no rest.

When treading the murky waters robbed me of strength, I sank to the bottom. I reveled in my anger at God, and wallowed in self-pity.

Drowning, I came to the end of myself, clawing my way out, and worried it was too late.

Precious One, it is never too late to turn back. Never.

Hebrews 13:6 (CSB), "I will never leave you or abandon you."

Did you hear that? He will never leave you nor abandon you. He will not give up on you. If you have chosen to jump out of the boat, though you may sink, He is there waiting. He will go to the depths of Sheol to save you.

"Where can I go to escape your Spirit? Where can I flee from your presence?

If I go up to heaven, you are there; if I make my bed in Sheol, you are there." Psalms 139:7&8 (CSB)

While I was running, He was pursuing me. Wooing me back into His arms.

If you are choosing rescue, choosing life, at this moment surrender all that you are to a loving, faithful God who will not leave you nor abandon you.

"For we know, brothers and sisters loved by God, that He has chosen YOU." 1Thessalonians 1:4 (CSB) (emphasis mine)

He has chosen you, holy and beloved. You are seen and known. You are pursued even to the depths of Hell.

He will rescue you.

You are loved.

Journaling Prompt

Have you fallen away from God?

What can you do today to make your way back to Him?

24 FREEDOM: CAUGHT IN THE NET

"For you are my rock and my fortress; you lead and guide me for your name's sake. You will free me from the net that is secretly set for me, for you are my refuge." Psalm 31:3-4 (CSB)

This passage of Scripture prompts me to ponder the nets that capture me.

David is pleading for protection from his enemies; the traps set out to snare him. This particular passage of Scripture became personal to me.

I am my own worst enemy. The nets that ensnare me are not from others, but those I have created.

I think of the words from Andrew Peterson's song, The Sower's Seed:

"Oh God I am furrowed like the field torn open like the dirt, and I know that to be healed I must be broken first."

For healing to come, I need to name the things that quickly ensnare me, dragging me under the weight of sin. Sin, that will break me if left unchecked.

- Approval seeking
- Perfectionism
- Control
- Fear
- Pride
- Greed
- Comparison

- A number on the scales
- Idolatry
- Gossip
- Discontentment

Do any of these feel familiar?

We come to His Word for nourishment, Living Water, guidance, and wisdom. We also come to the Word that our sin may be exposed. It is easier to take only the good and leave the bad, but that is not the way of God. Sin, unchecked, will kill and destroy our lives, separating us from God. That is a hard truth. As Christians, we sell the good stuff and cover up the hard conversations. We get uncomfortable at the mention of sin and the consequences that come with it.

"For my gaze takes in all their ways. They are not concealed from me, and their iniquity is not hidden from my sight." Jeremiah 16:17 (CSB)

"For I know your crimes are many and your sins innumerable." Amos 5:12a (CSB)

"If we say, 'We have no sin,' we are deceiving ourselves, and the truth is not in us." I John 1:8 (CSB)

Turning over the soil of my soul, spade in hand, I realize digging deeper would reveal more. I am cozy with many of the sins I was prompted to list. Too comfortable. Some, fought in the minute to minute, day to day of my life, while others lurk near the edges.

Deceiving ourselves is easy. Covering up, hiding our sin will cause more complications. When we bring our sin into the light, He is faithful and just to forgive us.

"Don't participate in the fruitless works of darkness, but instead expose them. For it is shameful even to mention what is done by them in secret. Everything exposed by the light is made visible." Ephesians 5:11-13 (CSB)

"If we confess, our sins, he is faithful and righteous to forgive us our sins and to cleanse us from all unrighteousness." I John 1:8-9 (CSB)

Carrying unconfessed sin traps and ensnares us in Satan's net. Life is hard, why do we want to add weight to already heavy bags? I do not.

I carry enough extra weight, living day to day with chronic illness.

What's the answer? How do we deal with the things that so easily ensnare us? How do we gain freedom?

- Shining Light on our sin.
- Confession
- Repentance
- Change
- Taking captive every thought, deed, and action to the Word of God.

When we do these, the net releases us from the entanglement of sin. We find freedom and healing begins. We can let the transgression go as God forgives.

"As far as the east is from the west, so far has he removed our transgressions from us." Psalm 103:12 (CSB)

"For you are my rock and my fortress; you lead and guide me for your name's sake. You will free me from the net that is secretly set for me, for you are my refuge." Psalm 31:3-4 (CSB)

Journaling Prompt

What habitual or unconfessed sin do you have in your life?

Are you willing to bring it out into The Light, confessing it to God?

25 HOARDER OR GIVER

Hoarder or giver? Do I clench tightly to the thing I am commanded to give away? The truth is, I have been a fat Christian. Hoarding what I know to be true, when I should be sharing.

"So my word that comes from my mouth will not return to me empty, but it will accomplish what I please and will prosper in what I send it to do." Isaiah 55:11 (CSB)

We were in a season of new: new community, new church family, a new way of life with chronic illness. I was desperately searching for my place in the midst of change. Longing to be embraced and to belong; to find my footing, a place to serve, while standing on weak legs.

It was during this time I heard two words that changed me, my way of thinking, and opened my eyes. "Fat Christians." I was offended, and nursing hurt feelings. I had spent the last year on the mountaintop with God, gripping the tattered edges of my life. Physically spent, spiritually filled, I could not reconcile the words, "fat Christians."

I turned to one of my favorite Bible stories where Peter and John heal a lame man.

"Now Peter and John were going up to the temple for the time of prayer at three in the afternoon. A man who was lame from birth was being carried there. He was placed each day at the temple gate called Beautiful, so that he could beg from those entering the temple. When he saw Peter and John, about to enter the temple, he asked for money. Peter, along with John, looked

straight at him and said, 'Look at us.' So he turned to them, expecting something from them.

But Peter said, 'I don't have silver or gold, but what I do have, I give you: In the name of Jesus Christ of Nazareth, get up and walk!' Then taking him by the right hand he raised him up, and at once his feet and ankles became strong. So he jumped up and started to walk, and he entered the temple with them - walking, leaping, and praising God." Acts 3:1-8 (CSB)

Turning Peter's words over in my heart, I begin to see, I am a hoarder with sealed lips, not sharing what God has done for me. With each missed opportunity to share, I had become a fat Christian.

I love Peter's words to the broken lame beggar, *"I don't have silver or gold, but what I do have, I give you."*

God has grown me since my time on the mountaintop with Him. I long to share what I have. I long to share what He has done for me.

In the busyness of everyday life, we blindly become a hoarder. Unwilling to miss checking off our list, or slowing down enough to offer what we do have. We are slowly getting fat.

It takes boldness and courage to share our faith and proclaim the Gospel. Transparency to share what God has done for us. We have been commanded to give, to share what we know and what He has done for us.

If not me or you, then who? Who feeds the hungry the Bread of Life? Who gives the thirsty Living Water. Who speaks words of life over the lame and dirty? Are we willing to callously step over them, feign ignorance, self-importance, or worse, pass judgment?

We are either a hoarder or a giver. Where do you fall?

"Jesus came near and said to them, 'All authority has been given to me in heaven and on earth. Go therefore, and make disciples of all nations, baptizing them in the name of the Father and of the Son and of the Holy Spirit, teaching them to observe everything I have commanded you. And remember, I am with you always, to the end of the age.'" Matthew 28:18-20 (CSB)

One generation will declare your works to the next and will proclaim your mighty acts. I will speak of your splendor and glorious majesty and your wondrous works. They will proclaim the power of your awe-inspiring acts, and I will declare your greatness." Psalms 145:4-6 (CSB)

"Even while I am old and gray, God, do not abandon me while I proclaim your power to another generation, your strength to all who come." Psalms 71:18 (CSB)

Journaling Prompt

Do you find it hard to share your story?

How can you change that?

Does it make it a difference that someone, possibly someone close to you, needs to hear your story?

26 LOOKING BEYOND THE CLOSED DOOR

Judging Others

Shouldn't there be grace for what lies beyond the closed door before judging others? Am I quicker to judge than to give grace?

On a recent shopping trip, I did not make it beyond the door before my haughtiness took over and I was passing judgment on those who looked different than me. The woman in her cloud covered pajamas and unkempt hair, the folks with offensive body odor whose list sent them down every aisle I needed to pass through. My good intentions to give grace and not judge faded fast.

It's not only the shopping trips. How many times do we sit in our seats at Sunday Worship, glancing around, passing judgment? We are the people who greedily take grace, yet withhold it from others. We seem to have attained some higher status by showing up clean smelling, well-kept, and dressed in our Sunday best.

We are receivers of grace; therefore, we are grace-givers.

If not, we should be. Giving grace is looking beyond the closed doors. Searching beyond what we can see, to the possible illness that sent the pajama-clad woman in search of medicine. The offensive body odor, perhaps homeless, with no place to bathe.

At first glance, I might appear inebriated, with shakes or withdrawals. If you look beyond the first obvious judgment, my disease causes severe vertigo; the ability to walk straight has long since left me. The shakes are not from withdrawals but from a yo-yo'ing blood pressure that never settles long in the right place. The dry mouth and slurred words from brain fog, which Dysautonomia causes. Meanwhile, I step into the door of Wal-mart and immediately begin to judge.

We are not the judge. We are meant to be the grace givers. We should be speaking life, whispering prayers, pouring out love, looking beyond the closed doors at what we cannot see. The cheating husband, the wayward child, addiction, illness, hopelessness, depression, so much more beyond our natural sight.

I pray for a gracious heart and in the next breath snap at a disruption. I pray for eyes to see beyond the closed doors and dirty clothes. I pray for a soul that does not judge. And still, I fail.

"Do not judge, so that you won't be judged. For you will be judged by the same standard with which you judge others, and you will be measured by the same measure you use. Why do you look at the splinter in your brother's eye but don't notice the beam of wood in your own eye? Or how can you say to your brother, 'Let me take the splinter out of your eye,' and look, there's a beam of wood in your own eye? Hypocrite! First take the beam of wood out of your eye, and then you will see clearly to take the splinter out of your brother's eye." Matthew 7:1-5 (CSB)

I pray for a heart that sees beyond the dirt, beyond the odor, to the broken spirit in need of grace. I pray for a soul that gives grace as I have been graced. I pray for a heart that loves big in hard places, and a heart that loves the unlovely.

Journaling Prompt

Is giving grace to the unlovely hard for you?

If so, what can you do to change that?

Is judgment your first response to the unlovely?

How can you change that?

27 RUN YOUR RACE

The Wilderness Marathon

"Therefore, since we also have such a large cloud of witnesses surrounding us, let us lay aside every hindrance and the sin that so easily ensnares us. Let us run with endurance the race that lies before us, keeping our eyes on Jesus, the source and perfector of our faith. For the joy that lay before him, he endured the cross despising the shame, and sat down at the right hand of the throne of God." Hebrews 12:1-2 (CSB)

I chose today's Scripture from Hebrews because I *was* a runner. I am a runner. When I was able to run, long distances were my favorite; they built endurance and they were challenging. I loved every moment and every step. My last physical race I fell flat on my face at mile two, passing out. That race has led to the most critical race in my life.

The Wilderness Marathon. Running through the unknown, through barren land and rocky terrain. A run without pointers and arrows to guide me, keeping me from getting lost. I did not sign up for The Wilderness Marathon, the wilderness found me. The unexpected knocked the wind from my lungs, tangled my feet, and forced me into a chair.

A new life, a new routine, a new race. Losing any semblance of control over my body and my life, flailing about in need of direction.

How in the unholy hard does one adjust their course? How can you change your course?

There was only one place to go, one Guide through The Wilderness Marathon.

Hebrews 12:1-2 (CSB) Laying aside every hindrance and sin that easily entangles.

For me that was control, accepting my weakness, learning to live outside of my comfort zone, and narrowing my boundaries.

Keeping my eyes on the Guide. In a regular marathon, cheerleaders and coaches are strategically placed along the way, encouraging, giving pep talks, and talking you through any negotiations you may be having with yourself, somewhere along mile eighteen.

In this case, God guided me, carried me when my feet could not. He wiped my tears, whispered strength into my soul. He fed me sustenance when I could not feed myself.

The cloud of witnesses. I would not have survived without my Sweet Man, soul sister, prayer warriors, family, and our community. Soup, banana bread, small gifts, cards, and books showed up at just the right time.

I could feel the hand of God wiping my tears as I wrestled through the wilderness. I felt His hand on my back pushing me forward when I could not move. His comfort in the scary unknown. I begged and pleaded for strength to live my story well.

He has given me so much more. Though this has been the hardest race of my life, I would not trade it for all the others, the races run and the ones not run. I can see the endurance He was building in me for this marathon.

It has been here in The Wilderness where He has become the Love of my life, my Sustainer, and Provider.

Journaling Prompt

Are you currently in your own Wilderness Place?

What things can you do to thrive in the hard?

Tammy L. Mashburn

28 GUIDE TO LIVING IN ABUNDANCE

"The Lord says, 'I will guide you along the best pathway for your life. I will advise you and watch over you.'" Psalms 32:8

When I look at the Israelites being led by the pillar of cloud by day and a pillar of fire by night, I confess to you, I'm a bit jealous. They were sent into the wilderness with a personal guide. Not just any guide, but The Guide.

God, the Creator of the Universe, creator of me and you.

On the run from the Egyptians, the Lord went ahead of the Israelites, making a way. Protecting them.

"The Lord went ahead of them. He guided them during the day with a pillar of cloud, and he provided light at night with a pillar of fire. This allowed them to travel by day or by night. And the Lord did not remove the pillar of cloud or pillar of fire from its place in front of the people. Exodus 13:21-22 (NLT)

I know the wilderness well and I'm thinking you may know a bit about it yourself. I've spent moments gazing at my life, searching for the pillar of cloud or the pillar of light.

As the Israelites, I have wandered in circles, peering at the negatives, the unholy hard, and overlooking The Guide. Overlooking my Guide. No, we don't have the pillar of cloud nor the pillar of fire, we have His Word.

We have His Word. His Word, a guide to all things and for all things. Every answer you will ever need is between the pages of His sacred text.

Every ounce of comfort you crave is between the pages.

The love you long for, between the pages.

The belonging you are missing, between the pages.

What falls between His sacred words cannot be found anywhere else.

But if you fail to open them, fail to search the words, you have missed the pillar of cloud and the pillar of fire.

"Your word is a lamp for my feet and a light on my path." Psalms 119:105

"I am weary from grief; strengthen me through your word." Psalm 119:28

"So my word that comes from my mouth will not return to me empty, but it will accomplish what I please and will prosper in what I send it to do." Isaiah 55:11 (CSB)

"For the word of God is living and effective and sharper than any double-edged sword, penetrating as far as the separation of soul and spirit, joints and marrow. It is able to judge the thoughts and intentions of the heart." Hebrews 4:12

"In the beginning was the Word, and the Word was with God, and the Word was God." John 1:1 (CSB)

What falls between these sacred pages cannot be found anywhere else.

When you read them, the Author is sitting with you. When applied to your life, they breathe life into your weary soul.

When you are looking for God and feel as if you have missed Him, He is the Word. When you say you cannot hear Him, all you need do, is open His Word.

The secret to everything you are longing for lies in His Word.

Just as the Israelites had a guide, you have a guide.

His Word is your guide to living life abundantly.

You will come to know His voice when you are spending time in His Word.

Journaling Prompt

He gave us His Word as our guide, are you using it?

Where do you turn to for guidance and wisdom if not His Word?

29 LIVING OUR FULLEST POTENTIAL

Faith that takes action will lead us to our fullest potential and lead us through a gateway of hope and into a place of rest.

"But whoever drinks from the water that I will give him will never get thirsty again. In fact the water I will give him will become a well of water springing up in him for eternal life." John 4:14 (CSB)

I turned the pages to Hosea, chapter two. Words jumped off the page as I prayed the words:

Lord, may your word dwell richly within me. Make me a tree that bears much fruit. I do not care to be a beautiful tree covered in leaves only. I long to be a bearer of fruit. Open my eyes to wondrous things from your instructions.

Hosea, the prophet was instructed by God to marry a prostitute named Gomer.

Warren Wiersbe, in his commentary, *Be Amazed*, said this of Hosea:

"But no prophet preached a more painful 'action sermon' than Hosea. He was instructed to marry a prostitute named Gomer, who subsequently bore him three children, and he wasn't even sure the last two children were fathered by him. Then Gomer left him for another man, and Hosea had the humiliating responsibility of buying back his own wife."

Faith that takes action leads us to our fullest life.

Several key verses grab my attention.

"Therefore, I am going to persuade her, lead her to the wilderness, and speak tenderly to her. There I will give her vineyards back to her and make the Valley of Achor into a gateway of hope.

There she will respond as she did in the days of her youth, as in the day she came out of the land of Egypt." Hosea 2:14-15 (CSB)

God used Hosea's marriage to Gomer as a spiritual picture of the Israelites prostituting themselves for other gods. Ouch! I am in awe of Hosea's obedience; I cannot help but wonder would I be willing to do the same?

Do I possess this all-in, surrendered obedience?

If I am to bear fruit, if His Word dwells richly within me, I have to be willing to live as Hosea. Hosea is a picture of surrendered obedience even in the hard things, in spite of the hard edges of his life. In a very public and humiliating way.

God used Hosea in a mighty way to show the Israelites they were worth going after. He is also speaking to us with this story, wooing and pursuing us away from evil and worthless idols.

We too are often enticed by worthless idols, wrapped up in glittery temptations.

Just as Hosea sought out Gomer, purchasing her again, God surrendered His one and only Son for you and me. We are bought and paid for with His blood.

The Valley of Achor was the valley of trouble, but choosing a life of faith leads us through a gateway of hope and into rest.

Journaling Prompt

Are we living to our fullest potential from this place?

Are we willing to live a faith that takes action?

30 DEEP ROOTS

"If you remain in me and my words remain in you, ask whatever you want and it will be done for you." John 15:7 (CSB)

The first half of my Christian life was spent skimming off the top of His Word, not digging deep, planting deep, or yielding a harvest. I can give you a myriad of reasons why, a plethora of excuses and justification. The bottom line is, I did not know how.

Coming from a legalistic background, making a list and checking it off came easy to me. I had a morning quiet time, a prayer journal, I read my Bible. I taught young girls Sunday School and led Women's Bible Studies. I dressed the part, acted the part, but my soul was a vast cavern of emptiness.

I was an imposter. An imposter who knew the right words to say, the right verses to share, encouraging others in their walk, and all the while, I was sinking.

You can only live by skimming the Word so long before the winds and waves of life knock you flat, sucking you under. That is exactly where I found myself when I turned away from God. Crying out, "How could you, Lord, when I am DOING all the right things?"

I was done and I was vocal about it. I found a box, tossed in my Bible study tools and commentaries, Bible Studies I had led and taught, along with the beloved Bible my Sweet Man had given me. Sealing the box, I sent him up the attic steps with it, and that is where 'the box' stayed for about four years.

Sealing God out of my life led to spending those years in the pit of Hell. (That's another book!) Suffice it to say, it was not pretty.

Not giving up on me, God pulled me from the pit. He was firm with me, but tender as well. Bandaging my wounds, whispering words of love into my empty soul. He pursued and beckoned, until I sent my Sweet Man back up the stairs to retrieve 'the box' containing my beloved Bible, and Bible study tools.

From that moment, I began to pray the words of *Psalm 37:4 (CSB): Take delight in the Lord, and he will give you your heart's desire.*

I wanted HIM to be my heart's desire.

He answered that prayer and many more as I began to be bold with my prayers. I wanted a deeper relationship with Him, to go deeper in His Word. I prayed that no matter what life slung my way, I would never turn from Him again. I prayed for deep roots, and a Kingdom harvest. That He would increase as I decrease. I prayed for "Even If" faith.

Shallow Christianity may look good on the outside, may even hold up for a little while. At the end of the day, without deep roots in Him and His Word, you will not make it.

Our relationship with Him must be deeply rooted, our love for Him must come before all other things and people.

Journaling Prompt

Would you consider your relationship with God, and His Word, shallow or deep?

What can you do to go deeper with Him?

31 FEEDING YOUR SOUL

Spending Time Alone with God

Feeding your soul means going to the banquet table.

"When Jesus heard about it, he withdrew from there by boat to a remote place to be alone." Matthew 14:13 (CSB)

Mornings in the Word is essential to me. Time in His Word and time alone with God is my lifeline, it is where I go to pour out my heart and feed my soul. I cannot, do not, want to do life any other way. It is everything to me because He is everything to me. It lights me up, stirs a fire in my belly, and makes me hungry for more.

I stumble from bedside to shower, to the coffee pot, and back to my desk. The air is chilled, I slip my wool-clad feet from Birkenstocks, and toss a fuzzy blanket across my lap. This place, my office, with opened Bible, journal and pens, becomes Holy Ground. I do not take it lightly. Sacred time invested in His Word will always yield return.

"So my word that comes from my mouth will not return to me empty, but it will accomplish what I please and will prosper in what I send it to do." Isaiah 55:11 (CSB)

When I am in a place of wrestling, a place of questioning, searching for answers, I may not get the answers I seek. But I can look back through the pages and trace God's hand in my life, and see His faithfulness.

"Ask, and it will be given to you. Seek, and you will find. Knock, and the door will be opened to you." Matthew 7:7 (CSB)

There are days when mere crumbs are served, and there are days of feasting. Small bites keep me going back for more. The more I seek, the more I find God.

If you are not already spending time alone with God, I want to encourage you to begin. Small beginnings, and consistency, will turn your investment of time into a banquet, a feast of words, guidance, and wisdom. Feeding your soul will give you the strength to feed those in your life.

Feeding your soul, feasting on His words, will move and guide you through your wilderness.

Journaling Prompt

How much time are you spending alone with God?

Are you praying for wisdom, knowledge, and understanding from His Word?

ABOUT THE AUTHOR

Tammy Mashburn is a writer suffering from a chronic neurological disease, Postural Orthostatic Tachycardia Syndrome, a form of Dysautonomia Disorder, and bone degeneration. Refusing to let suffering define her, she writes from the perspective of wilderness and not desperation.

A former marathon runner enjoying vigorous 25-mile morning runs, Tammy now refers to her POTS diagnosis as The Wilderness Marathon. This marathon is unlike any she's experienced yet has given her a perspective, which benefits her readers. On this journey she longs to encourage others in their race.

Writing from a place of chronic pain and everyday difficulties in the mundane, Tammy abides in, and relies on, her deep relationship with Jesus Christ and is committed to sharing her gifts of grace with her readers.

Tammy lives with her husband of thirty-plus years, referring to him as her Sweet Man, and one furry friend, Lola. Together they reside in their Wilderness

Place in the foothills of beautiful South Carolina.

Tammy's passion is to encourage women, teaching Sunday School, leading a women's small group at their church, and blogging. [Tammy can be found at tammylmashburn.com, where she shares gifts of grace several times each week. Email Tammy at tlmashburn@yahoo.com]

If you enjoyed this book or received value from it in any way, then I'd like to ask you to leave a review on Amazon. It would be greatly appreciated.

Mornings in The Word

Made in the USA
Columbia, SC
04 August 2018